Commercial Drone Services

Starting a Thriving UAV Business

Table of Contents

Chapter 1. Introduction

Unveiling the fascinating world of Unmanned Aerial Vehicles (UAVs), our Special Report on "Commercial Drone Services: Starting a Thriving UAV Business" offers unique insights and pragmatic advice for enterprising minds. This report will guide you through the rapidly emerging market, regulatory frameworks, and business opportunities related to commercial drone use. It is not drowned in complex tech jargon but rather a feasibly navigable guide unveiling profitability opportunities with UAVs. You will discover key strategies to set your drone business apart, yield high returns, and build a thriving enterprise. This report is an exciting journey into the future of business; your must-have guide to turning these high-flying instruments into a profitable venture. Propel your business ethics to new heights, quite literally! Let's navigate this promising airspace together.

Chapter 2. Understanding the Drone Market Landscape

The drone market greets with a dynamic landscape that is poised for remarkable growth in the coming years. Rapid advancements in technology combined with relaxed federal regulations are fueling this surge. In fact, the global drone market size is expected to reach $42.8 billion by 2025, according to a report by Grand View Research. Now more than ever, it's crucial that potential drone entrepreneurs understand this evolving environment comprehensively.

2.1. Exploring The Market Size & Potential Growth

The commercial drone market is segmented broadly into hardware, software and services. The hardware market comprises the sale of a variety of drones from small, handheld devices to larger, more technologically advanced UAVs. The software segment is categorized by analytical tools that provide insights from drone captured data. The services sector stands for drone service providers who offer specialized services like aerial photography or inspection services.

In the hardware sector, consumer drones currently constitute the majority of sales. On the other hand, it's the enterprise and service sectors that present the most substantial opportunities for growth. This is because businesses across various industries are increasingly recognizing the value that drone technology can bring to their operations, from improving safety in construction sites to revolutionizing delivery services.

2.2. Unveiling The Key Segments In Demand

The construction industry is one of the leading consumers of drone technology. There, drones offer unprecedented advantages in site safety, planning, and maintenance. Agriculture, too, is a burgeoning segment, employing UAVs to improve efficiency and yields through precision farming. Energy, mining, and insurance are also displaying growing interest in UAVs.

Mapping, surveying, and photography remain the heavy users of drones in terms of sheer volume – revolutionizing everything from wedding photography to real-estate marketing. Meanwhile, first responders and law-enforcement are adopting drones for missions inaccessible or hazardous to human pilots.

2.3. Regulatory Frameworks and Implications

Understanding the legal landscape is vital for establishing a drone business. Regulations, at a global level, are evolving, but often they form the most significant barrier for many enterprising players. In most countries, the types of applicable laws depend on several factors such as the size of the drone, its intended use, and the area where it will be operated.

In the US, for instance, the FAA regulates the commercial use of drones under Part 107, which lays down rules for drone registration, pilot certification, and operations. Meanwhile, in Europe, the European Union Aviation Safety Agency (EASA) has recently implemented a new regulatory framework to provide common rules throughout the EU member states.

Staying abreast of these regulations, and even anticipating their evolution, can offer a competitive edge. The expansion of regulations can open new opportunities for businesses that are ready to capitalize on them.

2.4. Technological Factors & Innovations

The technology behind drones continues to advance at a rapid pace. Improvements in areas such as battery life, camera quality, data processing capabilities, and artificial intelligence are continually expanding the range of services that commercial drones can offer.

Key innovations in the drone industry, like beyond visual line of sight (BVLOS) operations, are opening new possibilities for services such as long-distance inspections or drone deliveries. Simultaneously, improvements in automation and AI are pushing drones toward more autonomous and precise operations.

Another emerging trend is the use of drones in combination with other advanced technologies. For example, combining UAVs with 5G connectivity or IoT can offer expanded capabilities for data gathering, processing, and real-time communication.

2.5. Competitive Landscape & Strategies

Finally, understanding the competitive landscape is imperative for any aspiring drone entrepreneur. The drone industry is characterized by a combination of large tech firms, startups, and specialized drone companies.

By gaining a deep understanding of your competitors and the services they offer, you can find gaps in the market that your business can fill. Moreover, figuring out a unique selling proposition

(USP) for your services, whether it's cost-efficiency, service quality, or innovation, will set you apart from others in this competitive space.

Understanding this rapidly evolving drone market landscape is the first step to establishing a successful drone business. By recognizing and tapping into the potential opportunities, staying updated with regulatory changes, leveraging the latest technological advancements, and carving out a niche in the competitive market, you can build a thriving enterprise in the UAV industry.

Chapter 3. Commercial Applications of Drones: Current and Potential

While traditional methods of aerial surveying and surveillance remain mainstream, the advent of drones has disrupted numerous industries. Offering ingenuity and cost-effectiveness, drones operate in areas that are inaccessible, dangerous, or expensive for human personnel. This chapter explores the manifold commercial applications of drones, shedding light on existing implementations and prospective areas of exploration.

3.1. Surveying and Mapping

Drones play a pivotal role in the spatial data collection for surveying and mapping. Their capability to generate highly detailed cartographic data swiftly and economically outperforms traditional survey methods. With the integration of innovative technologies such as Geographic Information System (GIS) and Remote Sensing (RS), drones provide crucial topographical, geological, vegetation and other environmental information.

Data from drone surveys is extensively utilized to map property boundaries, infrastructure assessment, landform evaluation, flood risk management, and urban planning. Companies like DroneDeploy offer comprehensive drone surveying services, aiding industries from construction to agriculture.

Furthermore, adopting commercial drone services in surveying and mapping reduces field time, minimizes potential risks for personnel, and offers flexibility in scheduling and data collection.

3.2. Infrastructure Inspection

Routine inspection and maintenance of infrastructure such as telecommunication towers, pipelines, power lines, wind turbines, and solar panels are imperative yet perilous tasks. Drone technology has made this process significantly safer and more efficient.

Employing UAVs equipped with high-resolution cameras and infrared sensors, companies can perform regular inspections without endangering human life. Drones can swiftly traverse huge expanses of infrastructure, capturing images in minute detail. British Petroleum (BP), for instance, uses drones to inspect pipelines and oilfields, saving invaluable time and enhancing safety.

3.3. Precision Agriculture

Modern agricultural practices are increasingly integrating drones for a wide spectrum of applications. Precision farming, crop monitoring, livestock tracking, and irrigation management are some areas greatly impacted.

Drones armed with multispectral sensors capture actionable crop health data, helping farmers identify issues early on. This precise, real-time information enables farmers to focus resources precisely where needed, improving yield and sustainability. Additionally, drones can assist in automating the tedious task of livestock tracking, saving manpower and time.

3.4. Delivery Services

Amazon shook the world with its ambitious 'Prime Air' plan to utilize drones for faster deliveries. Several companies, including Alphabet's Wing and UPS, now have approved drone delivery trials. While regulatory complications persist, drones hold prospect for swift, eco-friendly, and cost-effective last-mile deliveries.

Drones can carry small parcels and medical supplies efficiently across complex routes, bypassing traffic congestion and inaccessible terrains. In the health sector, drones are already delivering life-saving medicines, vaccines, and medical supplies in remote or disaster-hit areas.

3.5. Real Estate

Drones enable breath-taking aerial shots, providing impressive panoramic views for real estate marketing. They provide easy access to rooftops and other inaccessible areas, enabling more detailed home inspections. This new viewpoint offers potential buyers unique insights into the property, bolstering real estate marketing to previously unattainable levels.

Looking towards the future, drones will be a key tool in a multitude of industries, from emergency services for immediate disaster response to advanced scientific research. Technological advancements and relaxation in regulatory constraints will continue paving the way for innovative commercial drone usage.

3.6. Legal Considerations

As drone technology shapes futuristic business avenues, it also presents complex legal challenges. Diverse regulations govern drone usage, including restrictions on drone weight, flying height, proximity to urban areas or airports, and much more. Being abreast with changes in fast-evolving drone laws and ensuring compliance will be critical for commercial drone stakeholders. Understanding these laws can help businesses avoid penalties and protect their operations.

The potential of drones in the commercial realm is vast and boundless. From startups to corporate giants, understanding the depth and breadth of opportunities offered by drones can revolutionize thinking, operations, and business strategies. As the sky is not the limit for drones, let's soar high into the future, grasping new horizons of innovation and profitability.

Chapter 4. Regulations and Compliance: Staying Afloat in the Airspace

Regulation and compliance have etched themselves as indispensable factors of the commercial drone industry. Navigating this aerial space isn't a feat achievable impulse or intuition; rather, it's stringently controlled and carefully regulated by legal frameworks to ensure safety, privacy, and harmony.

4.1. The ABCs of Regulation

Regulatory bodies worldwide have framed specific rules, harmoniously balanced between unlocking innovative possibilities and ensuring safety. In the United States, the governing entity is the Federal Aviation Administration (FAA), whereas in Europe, it is the European Union Aviation Safety Agency (EASA). Each body has its own set of rules and qualification criteria for businesses to legally operate drones.

Consider that the FAA requires commercial drone operators in the U.S. to hold a Remote Pilot Certificate under the Part 107 rule. This rule mandates navigational knowledge testing every two years. Similar, yet distinct, regulations prevail in different geographies, and staying updated is essential for smooth navigation through this legal airspace.

4.2. Compliance: The Make-or-Break Factor

Where UAV operation is concerned, non-compliance costs more than a hefty fine. It can jeopardize your entire business credibility, potentially leading to operational limitations or even downright grounding.

Most regulatory bodies require drone businesses to complete rigorous tests and adhere to specified rules for drone operational altitude, flight paths, speed, and time of operation (usually during daylight). Further, strict adherence to operating in specific zones, reporting accidents, routine maintenance, and insurance is also obligatory.

4.3. Understanding Part 107

For American stakeholders, understanding Part 107 regulations is paramount. Under this, businesses can fly drones weighing less than 55 lbs during the daytime and within the pilot's visible line of sight without the necessity for an airspace waiver. The operator must pass an initial aeronautical knowledge test at an FAA-approved knowledge testing center or hold a Part 61 pilot certificate.

Treading upon these grounds, with ongoing incremental changes, signifies successful navigation through the legal corridors of your drone business.

4.4. Drone Registration

Mandatory drone registration is a common regulatory provision worldwide. In the EU, all drones must be registered with the National Aviation Authority. Similarly, drones that weigh more than 0.55 lbs (250 g) and less than 55 lbs (25 kg) must be registered with the FAA before they can be flown outdoors in the U.S.

4.5. Privacy Laws

While it's crucial to comply with the governing bodies' guidelines by a thread, one also needs to respect individual privacy laws. Straying into personal spaces, even unintentionally, can have severe legal repercussions. Legal literacy regarding privacy is a must-have virtue for a UAV operator.

4.6. Keeping Up with Changes

Regulations are never stagnant; they evolve with the industry. It's essential to keep an eye on these changes, understanding their implications on your business, and adapting accordingly. Membership in drone industry organizations and attending seminars, webinars, and other resources can ensure you stay afloat.

4.7. Ensuring Safety

Beyond regulatory adherence, building a culture of safety in your business is integral. It's imperative to develop safety checklists, contingency plans, schedules for routine drone inspection, and thorough record-keeping protocols. Training your employees on these safety practices would enhance your credibility, increase profitability and longevity.

4.8. Insurance

Securing insurance, though not always mandatory, is often essential to protect your business from financial loss due to a mishap or accident involving your drone. Besides, insurance might also become a selling point for your services and bring an edge to your business proposal.

In essence, the success of your drone business quintessentially hinges upon regulatory adherence and compliance. The better you navigate the regulatory airspace, the smoother your business journey.

Chapter 5. Essential Equipment: Starting Your Drone Fleet

Selecting the right equipment is imperative in starting your drone fleet. There are numerous factors to deliberate, including your specific business needs, customizability, durability, and the quality of the camera. Furthermore, crucial accessories—such as extra batteries, sturdy carry cases, and insurance—cannot be overlooked.

5.1. Drone Choices

There are various types of UAVs to choose from, and it's crucial to select the one that best suits the nature of your work. For instance, Multi-Rotor drones are ideal for aerial photography, real estate, farming, and inspections due to their stabilization features. Fixed-Wing drones can cover long distances for map charting or surveillance.

For those starting their journey in establishing a commercial UAV business, here are some drone models worth considering:

1. DJI Phantom 4 Pro: Contender for the best all-around drone, the Phantom 4 Pro offers excellent flight time, 4K video recording, and a suite of security features.

2. Parrot Anafi: This light and collapsible drone is easy to transport and offers 4K video, a 25-minute flight time, and a 180-degree vertical-turn camera.

3. Yuneec Typhoon H Pro: A hexacopter distinguished by its high stability in wind and 6 rotor safety. It can capture 4K video and high-resolution stills with the integrated gimbal.

Remember, the choice of drone isn't just about the cost or camera quality. It must also take into consideration support, maintenance, and after-sales service availability.

5.2. UAV Accessories

Base purchases should include an extra battery, drone case, memory cards, and drone insurance.

1. Extra Battery: Maximize your flight time and productivity in the field by having extra battery packs.

2. Drone Case: Moving expensive equipment demands protection. Consider a case that protects against the roughest situations and weather.

3. Memory Cards: The quality of memory cards is essential for storing crucial mission data and high-quality video footage.

4. Drone Insurance: With high costs associated with drone repair, insurance becomes indispensable.

5.3. Customizing Your Drone

Capabilities of your drone can be further enhanced with additions such as:

1. First Person View (FPV) Goggles: these goggles provide a drone pilot with a first-person view of where the drone is heading.

2. GPS Mapper: It enables the accurate tracking and geotagging of areas covered and images captured.

3. Additional Sensors: Apart from the cameras, equipment like LIDAR, infrared sensors, thermal sensors enhance the capabilities of drones and help in more accurate data capturing and analysis.

5.4. Obtaining Your Drone License

Unless you're flying your drone solely as a hobby, a drone license, also known as a Part 107 Remote Pilot Certificate, is mandatory in the USA. This necessitates passing an FAA test about drone operation, airspace classification, and emergency procedures.

It is equally essential for you to know the limitations set by the FAA, such as not flying above 400 feet in altitude or at night, and not operating a drone from a moving vehicle.

5.5. Maintenance and Repair

Regular maintenance involves checking for damage to the blades, ensuring the batteries are fully charged, and watching for any software updates needed. A preventative maintenance schedule is recommended, and compulsory before every flight, to fix minor issues before they escalate into significant problems.

Technical skills for basic maintenance and repairs are essential to keep your drone in good condition and to potentially save costs on minor fixes. Formal training is often an overlooked aspect, but it is a key to longevity and reliability of the fleet.

Launching a successful drone business involves much more than buying a drone and selling your services. It requires the right equipment, skills, and planning to stay competitive in this rapidly growing market. Equip yourself with the right tools, knowledge, and skills, and your journey towards building a prosperous drone business will be a smoother flight.

Chapter 6. Operating Instructions: Mastering Flight and Navigation

Operating UAVs efficiently requires mastering two crucial aspects: flight and navigation. These skills are directly proportional to the safety and effectiveness of drone operations.

6.1. Understanding UAV Controls

First, let's start with the basics of UAV controls. Most commercial drones are quadcopters and have four main controls:

1) Throttle: This lifts the drone off the ground by increasing or decreasing the power to the motors. 2) Pitch: This makes your drone move forward and backward. 3) Roll: This moves your drone left or right. 4) Yaw: This rotates the drone clockwise or anticlockwise.

Understanding these controls is vital to operate drones effectively. However, knowing the controls is one thing, and using them efficiently is another. It requires a lot of practice and patience.

6.2. Practice Makes Perfect

Start by practicing in an open area away from obstacles. Remember to always keep the drone in sight and avoid flying it too far away.

1) Start with throttle control: Increase it slowly until the drone lifts off the ground. Practice maintaining a steady height. Then, practice landing safely. 2) Move to pitch and roll: Once you get a hang of it, start using pitch and roll together to move your drone in a specific direction. 3) Master Yaw: Finally practice using yaw along with other

controls. This can get a bit tricky as it changes the orientation of the drone.

As an exercise, try to mark an aerial square pathway and aim to fly your drone along this pathway.

6.3. Importance of Simulators

Training with UAV simulators cannot be overstressed. They provide a risk-free environment to practice your skills before getting your hands on an actual drone. A majority of these simulators offer realistic flying scenarios, challenging weather conditions, and all-important crash simulations, which are invaluable for any UAV operator. Try different simulators available in the market, and invest in one that suits your needs the best.

6.4. Navigating with GPS

In commercial operations, merely manual control is not enough, and that's where GPS comes into play. GPS allows you to pre-program your flight route, making operations more efficient and precise.

1) Waypoint Navigation: You can create a route of waypoints, which your drone will follow. Use this for surveying large areas or for regular inspections. 2) Follow Me: Here, your drone follows a GPS transmitter, usually in your controller or smartphone. It's helpful in videography where you need to follow a subject. 3) Return to Home: In this mode, your drone returns to its launch point if it loses connection with your controller or if the battery is running low.

Remember to always maintain a comprehensive database of your flight logs. Analyze them regularly to improve your operations, and use them as evidence if necessary.

6.5. Beyond the Basics

As you gather function and finesse, you should consider learning advanced techniques like:

1) Bank Turns: A technique for turning the drone smoothly by rolling and yawing at the same time. 2) Orbiting: Making the drone fly in a circular path around a subject, which is particularly effective for filming. 3) Flips and Rolls: More for hobbyist fliers, but learning such maneuvers improves your control over your drone.

Remember, while these are essential, mastering the drone's primary controls remain paramount.

Operating a UAV is both an art and science. Master it, and the sky becomes your canvas. While you start with basic controls, making them second nature requires diligence. Polish your skills with simulators, leverage GPS for navigation, and always push your boundaries, drawing from a safe and secure foundation. This chapter serves as a guide in the UAV operator's journey, paving the path from novice to expert. Evolve with your UAV and soar to higher levels of skill, safety, and efficiency. On this exhilarating journey, always remember your responsibilities as a UAV operator, and maintain the safety of the airspace.

Chapter 7. Insurance and Safety Measures for Commercial Drones

Understanding the necessity and significance of proper insurance for maintaining UAV operations is imperatively crucial. It provides a safety net for your business, sums up your serious commitment towards professionalism, and showcases your ethical predispositions.

7.1. Liability Insurance for Commercial Drones

Liability insurance is arguably the most critical protection you need as a drone entrepreneur. In most countries, liability insurance for commercial drone operators is mandatory. It covers you if your drone damages someone else's property or causes personal injury.

Keep in mind that this cover can range from one to several million dollars, primarily depending on the risks involved with your operations and the environment in which you operate. Naturally, filming a grand wedding in an open park would typically involve substantially less risk than conducting a high-quality site survey for a nuclear power plant!

Another essential factor is understanding that these policies usually cover only the so-called "flight time". From the moment your drone takes off to the instance it lands, you are covered. Anything happening before or after this falls into a different category.

7.2. Ground Risks and Hull Insurance

Hull insurance covers your drone and associated equipment but it doesn't offer the scope that liability insurance does. It's either an add-on or a completely different policy altogether. If your drone gets damaged in transit or stolen from your premises, hull insurance provides the financial backup to get you back in the air.

Although not always specifically required, it embodies a wise step towards complete protection. It is a worthy contemplation, especially if your equipment includes high-value drones or specialized attachments such as high-resolution camera equipment or cutting-edge sensors.

7.3. Additional Coverage: Personal Injury and Invasion of Privacy

Aside from the physical damages, it's important to acknowledge that when operating drones, there are more abstract risks involved. If your drone operations lead to a personal injury that isn't physical - invasion of privacy, psychological trauma, or alike, some policies will cover these. This kind of insurance is typically taken along with liability insurance.

7.4. Insurance Based on Proficiency

One innovative approach to drone insurance is "pay as you fly" coverage. Some companies offer this policy based on the operator's skill level, the complexity of the operation, the environment, and other risk factors. You can get insured on a short-term basis, like for a single day, which can prove cost-effective if your drone operations are infrequent.

7.5. Obtaining Drone Insurance

When applying for drone insurance, insurers will typically ask you for a lot of information. They'll want specifications of your drone, details about your operations, your volume of business, and records of any past claims or accidents. You may also need to provide evidence of your competency, such as a pilot's license or a drone training course completion.

Chapter 8. Setting Up Safety Measures

Having proper drone insurance doesn't mean you can ignore safety measures. Instead, implementing robust safety protocols reduces the risk of incidents that could see you relying on your insurance. Furthermore, showing insurers that you take safety very seriously might also lower your premiums.

8.1. Creating a Safety Checklist

A safety checklist is a practical tool for ensuring that every precaution is made before each flight. Your checklist should include checks for equipment, weather, bystander safety, and any permissions needed for the flight. Regularly maintaining your checklist and ensuring that it is followed rigorously will build a positive safety culture within your organization.

8.2. Understanding Local Regulations and No-fly Zones

Regulatory compliance is essential to ensure safe and successful drone operations. Always familiarize yourself with the latest drone laws in your operational jurisdictions. These might include height restrictions, no-fly zones, and drone registration requirements.

Not only will meeting these regulations keep you on the government's good side, but it also helps to mitigate risks. For example, operating in restricted airspace without correct permissions increases the likelihood of in-flight collisions.

8.3. Implementing a Safety Management System

A systematic approach to managing safety, including the necessary organizational structures, accountabilities, policies, and procedures is vital. As your drone business grows, you might need to look at safety management systems, safety audits, and further skills training.

8.4. Emergency Preparedness

No matter how prepared you are, accidents might happen. Rather than hoping they won't, be ready when they do. Plan for emergencies, train for them, and know what to do when things go wrong. This ranges from knowing how to conduct an emergency landing, to responding to a data breach, to communication in the event of an accident.

Incorporating safety measures and proper insurance is a symbiotic way of safeguarding your UAV business. It's about staying ahead of the curve, keeping abreast with operational risks and advancements, and assuring a well-rounded, professional, and successful commercial drone service.

Chapter 9. Marketing Strategies for Your Drone Business

Developing and implementing strategic marketing plans for a drone business is essential to its success. With an effective marketing strategy, you can sustainably grow your customer base, increase your profits, and set yourself apart from your competitors. This guide will provide you extensive insights and practical recommendations for formulating cost-effective and result-driven marketing strategies tailored particularly for Unmanned Aerial Vehicles (UAV) industry.

9.1. Identifying Your Target Market

The first step to crafting an effective marketing strategy is identifying your target market. While it's tempting to say that your products or services appeal to everyone, a winning strategy is always geared towards a specific group or audience. Market segmentation in the drone industry could be based on factors such as:

- Users' Skil Level: Novice, Intermediate, or Pro

- Application Areas: Surveillance, Surveying, Photography, Videography, Agriculture, or Delivery

Take time to understand your ideal customer. Know what they want, what they value, and what problems your UAV services can solve for them. This focused approach makes your marketing efforts efficient and effective.

9.2. Understanding Your Competitors

As the drone industry is becoming increasingly crowded, understanding your competitors is paramount. Competitor analysis allows you to understand their strengths, weaknesses, and strategies. This information, in turn, helps you frame your Unique Selling Proposition (USP) that differs your offerings from theirs.

Be thorough in understanding their price structures, customer service approach, technology, marketing efforts, and performance. Use this information to recognize gaps you can use to your advantage.

9.3. Developing a Unique Selling Proposition

Your USP is what sets you apart from your competition. To identify your USP, ask yourself:

- What makes your drone services unique?

- Why should customers choose your services over the competition?

- How does your approach, technology, or experience make a difference?

Make your USP the lead message in your marketing efforts, and reinforce it with every interaction with your customers.

9.4. Creating a Brand Identity

Your brand is more than just your logo or tagline – it's everything that people think of when they hear your business name. It gives your business an individualistic appeal in the crowded drone market. Your brand should reflect the essence of your business, your values, and your promise to your customers.

An impactful brand identity can foster trust and commitment among your potential customers. Keep in mind that everything from your website to your business cards and from your online advertisements to your customer service needs to reinforce your brand values.

9.5. Building an Online Presence

In today's digitally connected world, an online presence is not an optional add-on to your marketing strategies but rather a critical necessity. The extent of your online presence can vary based on your objectives, resources, and target audience, but at the minimum, it should include:

- Website: A professionally-designed, user-friendly, and informative website can provide your prospective customers with essential information.

- Social Media: Platforms like Facebook, Instagram, and LinkedIn offer cost-effective ways to engage with your target audience.

- Search Engine Optimization (SEO): Effective SEO strategies can help your business appear on top of search results, increasing your visibility among potential customers.

9.6. Utilizing Content Marketing

Content marketing can establish you as a thought leader in the drone industry and foster trust among your customers. Regularly develop and share relevant content via your website, blog, and social media channels. This content can include blog posts, infographics, videos, or webinars that provide value to your audience and subtly promote your services.

9.7. Engaging in Email Marketing

Email marketing is a highly effective digital marketing strategy for sending emails to prospects and customers. Building an email list and regularly sending out newsletters and promotional offers can boost engagement and keep your brand on top of mind.

9.8. Measuring Your Success

Success in marketing isn't just about doing; it's also about measuring. Keep track of Key Performance Indicators (KIPs) that align with your business goals. These could include the number of new leads generated, conversion rates, customer retention rates, or return on investment (ROI).

Implementing these marketing strategies can give your UAV business a competitive edge. Keep refining your strategies based on your learning and market dynamics to stay ahead. Remember, the race is not always to the swiftest but to those who keep moving.

Chapter 10. Revenue Streams in the Drone Business

Understanding the potential revenue streams is an integral part of any business, including when starting a UAV enterprise. To make the most out of your investment, it's critical to explore multiple channels where income can be generated, taking into account the ever-evolving regulations and market demands.

10.1. Services Offered

Drones have been significantly versatile, proving valuable across different sectors. Below are some of the services a drone business can offer:

1. **Photography/Videography**: The most recognizable use of drones commercially has been in the field of photography and videography. This extends to different sectors such as real estate, film production, and events like weddings or corporate functions.

2. **Precision Agriculture**: Drones fitted with multispectral sensors can help farmers monitor crop health and optimize resources, providing significant opportunities in the agricultural sector.

3. **Inspection Services**: Drones can be used for inspections in industries like construction, oil & gas, and infrastructure, offering cheaper and safer alternatives to traditional methods.

4. **Survey/Mapping**: Remote sensing capabilities of UAVs often come handy in the field of surveying, mapping and geospatial data collection.

5. **Delivery services**: With proper licensing and equipment, UAVs can be used as delivery mechanisms for small items, creating opportunities for last-mile logistics.

10.2. Pricing Strategy

After identifying the services offered by your business, it's crucial to determine an appropriate pricing strategy. Each drone service can be priced differently according to variables such as the time taken for each operation, the complexity of the task, and the equipment used.

Fixed-rate pricing per project can be one option, including labor cost, equipment cost, post-production tasks, and other expenses. This pricing strategy gives clients predictability and ease of budgeting.

Alternatively, an hourly rate can be adopted. The price will then factor in the time taken for pre-flight site inspections, material prep, actual flying time, and post-production tasks.

10.3. Recurring Revenue

Another stream to consider is securing recurring revenue. This model ensures predictable and steady income from contracts where drone services are required regularly. Industries such as agriculture, infrastructure monitoring, or real estate may be interested in such services.

Recurring revenue strategies can be divided into committed recurring revenue (such as contracts for a fixed period) and flexible recurring revenue (like a pay-as-you-go model). Deciding what suits your business depends on the services you offer and market conditions.

10.4. Selling Equipment and Accessories

In addition to services, selling drone-related equipment and accessories is another profitable stream. Items can range from drones of different specifications and spare parts to additional gear like specialized cameras or sensors that can be attached to drones.

Moreover, providing drone training and education can be a lucrative spin-off of your main service provision. As drone use proliferates, more professionals and individuals are keen to learn how to handle these machines responsibly and effectively.

10.5. Partnerships

Reaching out and forming strategic alliances with other companies can create opportunities for revenue sharing. Partnerships with businesses in construction, real estate, agriculture, or event planning can spur regular project engagements and revenue.

In conclusion, multiple revenue streams can lead to sustainable and robust income generation for your drone business. Embrace the diversity that UAVs offer and be strategic about the services you offer, pricing, and partnerships for success in the long run. Leveraging these streams with a strong understanding of your customer's needs, remaining adaptable with regulatory changes, and continuous innovation in technology is the key to a thriving UAV business.

Chapter 11. Case Studies: Successful Commercial Drone Services

With the booming popularity of Unmanned Aerial Vehicles (UAVs) businesses, many success stories abound. Herein, we dissect the case studies of high-profile businesses that have successfully incorporated commercial drone services.

11.1. Precision Hawk: Leaders in Drone Farming

Precision Hawk, a North Carolina based startup, was established in 2010. The company uses UAVs to collect data, easing the decision-making process for farmers. Detailed aerial images, analysis of plant health, prediction of crop yields, and efficient scouting reports are some of the services they offer.

While most drone companies focus on equipment sales, Precision Hawk prioritizes data collection and interpretation, helping clients enact informed decisions about their crops. Through Precision Analytics, they offer an AI-powered visual intelligence platform that transforms raw data into actionable knowledge. The success of Precision Hawk lies in its unique approach to using UAVs, with a diversified array of industries served, including agriculture, energy, insurance, and government.

11.2. Zipline: Saving Lives with UAVs

Zipline, founded in 2014, took an entirely different path. They view drones as a means to expedite critical medical supplies to remote areas. The company boasts a successful operation in Rwanda, a mountainous country where many regions are inaccessible during the rainy season. Zipline's drones allow for quicker delivery of blood and vaccines, making a significant impact on emergency medical situations.

Zipline capitalizes on UAV technology's potential to respond rapidly to critical needs. Their success speaks volumes about the ability to leverage drones for social causes, highlighting the significant societal impact commercial drone services can achieve.

11.3. Flirtey: Revolutionizing Fast-food Delivery

Flirtey, a Nevada-based startup, ventured into drone technology with an interesting perspective: deliver goods to consumers via drones. Partnering with Domino's in New Zealand, they accomplished the world's first pizza delivery by drone in 2016. The demonstration showed that UAVs could be a viable option for reducing the delivery times in the consumer industry.

By reshaping the face of traditional delivery systems, Flirtey taps into an untapped market - customers valuing speed and convenience. Their innovative approach potentially could reinvent the delivery sector in upcoming years.

11.4. Drone Deploy: Offering Drone Data Solutions

Drone Deploy, a San Francisco-based industry-leading drone software company, takes it to another level. Specialising in aerial mapping and 3D modeling, their platform assists in gathering, managing, and interpreting drone data. They cater extensively to agricultural needs, construction site mapping, mining operations, and other ventures that require detailed mapping services.

Drone Deploy realizes the potential drone data has in improving operational efficiency. Their successful, technology-based solutions give an edge to industries, pinpointing the importance of drones in the data management landscape.

11.5. Skyward: Streamlining Drone Operations

Skyward, a Verizon company, provides end-to-end drone operational solutions. Their cloud-based software helps businesses manage drone deployments, making it easier to navigate complex airspace regulations. They provide real-time airspace maps, safety risk assessment, and flight performance tracking.

Skyward's strategic move to simplify drone usage for businesses showcases a crucial aspect of commercial drone services: not just producing drone technology, but also making it practical for different industries.

These success stories underline how commercial drone services can diversify and revolutionize various sectors. From delivering pizza to saving lives, from analyzing crop health to streamlining drone operations, UAVs present exciting possibilities. However, central to these success stories is the recognition that the value of UAVs lies not just in the technology but in understanding the application of this technology to solve real-world challenges.

Chapter 12. Future Outlook: Emerging Trends in the Drone Industry

Innovation has always been at the forefront of any revolution, and the drone industry is no exception. Companies across the globe are pushing the boundaries of what's possible with Unmanned Aerial Vehicle (UAV) technology. Let's take a closer look at the future.

12.1. Advancements in Technology

With every passing year, newer and more advanced drones are hitting the market. These are equipped with enhanced features and extended capabilities such as longer flight times, better sensors, improved imaging systems, and intelligent flight modes.

Increased Battery Life and Flight Range: As technology advances, so does the power systems of UAVs. Companies are now producing drones with more extended battery life, allowing for longer flight times. This opens up possibilities for drone usage in areas such as exploration or long-haul deliveries. Additionally, with developments in signal technology and remote controls, the flight range is continually increasing, providing drones with a broader field of operation.

Improved Sensors and Imaging Systems: Drone technology is making significant strides in sensor and imaging systems. From high-definition cameras to infrared sensors, lidar, and even radar-based sensors, the options for capturing data are ever-increasing. These advanced imaging systems are not only helping capture better aerial footage but also enabling the use of drones in various fields such as inspections, surveillance, and mapping.

Artificial Intelligence Integration: AI and machine learning are being integrated into the drone feature set, allowing for a host of smart functionalities. These include automatic detection and avoidance of obstacles, intelligent tracking, and autonomous navigation. Drones equipped with AI can even perform complex operations such as roof inspections, identifying defects and anomalies without human intervention.

12.2. Expanding Applications

Innovative drone applications are continually emerging, covering a broad spectrum from entertainment to life-saving missions.

Ecommerce Deliveries: Companies like Amazon and UPS are experimenting with using drones for the delivery of goods. This method can speed up the delivery process, reaching customers in a shorter amount of time. Currently, the primary challenge lies in regulatory approval and logistical issues such as limited payload capacity and short battery life.

Emergency Responders: Drones are being increasingly utilized for emergency response. They help fire departments assess the extent of fires, provide live video feeds to disaster management teams, and help search and rescue operations by reaching places inaccessible to humans.

Agriculture: Farmers are using drones with multispectral sensors to monitor crop health and development, identify pest issues, and assess irrigation problems. They can apply fertilizers and pesticides precisely where required, limiting waste and reducing the environmental impact.

12.3. Regulatory Developments

However, the fast-paced growth in drone technology and

applications also requires proper governance and suitable policies.

Developing Comprehensive Laws: As drones become more ubiquitous, drafting comprehensive laws that address all aspects of drone use becomes critical. Factors such as privacy concerns, safety issues, and compliance with airspace rules need to be comprehensively covered in these laws.

Global Standardization: The implementation of standardized global rules for drone operation can provide a boost to the industry. These standards would provide a clear framework for operations, ensuring safety and increasing the public's confidence in drone technology.

12.4. Conclusion

The future of the drone industry undoubtedly holds a myriad of opportunities. As we approach a time where drones may become as common as smartphones, it is important to understand these future trends. These trends not only present us with a view of the upcoming improvements in drone technology but also make us aware of the challenges that lay ahead. Embracing these changes will be key to making the most out of this exciting industry. However, it will be a journey laden with complex regulatory requirements and technical hurdles. With careful planning, strategic investments, and innovative thinking, these obstacles can be overcome, making way for a thriving drone-based business.